A Gathering of Suns

Poems of the Ukrainian War and Diaspora

A Gathering of Suns

Poems of the Ukranian War and Diaspora

Murray Pura

Raven Croaks Publishing, San Bernardino

Raven Croaks Publishing, San Bernardino

Printed in the United States of America
First Edition 2022
ISBN 978-1-957743-03-5

Editor Suzanne Deshchidn
Interior design by Marvin Brauer
Cover Mary Rumford

www.ravencroaks.com

this book of poetry is dedicated to the memory of
Roman and Anna Pura of Lviv, Ukraine

Table of Contents

Part I: I thought as a child

Part II: I put away childish things

Part III: through a glass darkly

Milwaukee: American Volunteer

treading the night
war house 2022
black and bitter
no great loss
we are fighting on another street now

Vasyl:Ukranian Army

a perfect target
Marlboro Reds
we were born for this
smoke
blood roots
it rises at one end of the heavens

Yana:Ukranian Army

blackest night
the rings of Saturn
gone to graveyards
jigsaw

Myrrh:Canadian Volunteer

Part IV: face to face

I thought as a child

a ghost

the photograph was smaller
than my hand my hand
small as an eleven
year old's hand can be
when born too soon and
illness unwinds
the spread of his bones

white gray black and silver
the woman stared a stare
that cut me apart
eyes long ago in a skull in skin
too soon hazel eyes fell into
a hole backhoed from
hard earth stone buffalo bone

diesel dust and dirt
my aunt ending
in machinery and fuel
frost snowfall the

universal dark
but the photograph
outlived her eyes

who is she
why does she look like
she came from a grave
"do not talk," my father warns
"she just came for
Sunday dinner she is
at the table your Aunt Zaya

"the war the long ago war
she survived the war of
burning tanks burning wheat
burning skies burning ground
she is a survivor of the war
that burned Ukraine black
and turned every sunflower to dusk

"she was a prisoner
the Nazis took her

worked her soul to the bone

she looks far into that camera

for what she left in America

and Canada to help Stalin

build a world of peace and grace

"Stalin betrayed her

took her farmers

into the mud the Nazis came

and struck down all who

cried for liberty she lost her

husband and son your uncle and

cousin the guns stopped their hearts"

"it is not Aunt Zaya

it is not her eyes," I said

"the black silver white grey

is not her skin or face"

I sat across from her

at the table and looked into

her smile that American Sunday

I saw the smile did not smile

the eyes did not see
they were through me
and past me and many
miles beyond me on the
way to a country a husband
a son that did not exist

she asked me about school
said I was taller
I moved the peas about
on my plate and answered
with the shortest words
I could no longer be sure who
it was that sat across the Sunday
table from me where she was
going and where she would take
me if I let her kiss my cheek
smooth my hair grip my hand
even if she did it softly
like a ghost

colors

I held my first Easter egg

my aunt crouching over my shoulder

afraid I would drop it

the lines and angles bewildered me

some ran straight and some curved

some had the flow of tap water

others were a knife

the colors I could not comprehend

some looked bold and some soft

some as bright as sky or blood spots

others were a night

I handed the egg to my aunt

and asked what the puzzle of

lines and colors meant

Ukraine she said

assimilate 1

they would begin cold
at the great table in
the dining room Sundays

two sisters
ignoring one another
plucking at their food

one sister talking to us
the other a frozen fury
refusing to speak with anyone

because her sister had been invited
finally they give words to each other
choosing to get on with it

one quietly
the other in harsh cuts
quickly they switch to Ukrainian

collapse into fierce sledge and
boulder argument I could never
understand because I was not

meant to understand they knew
no one else at the table spoke
the language of Kyiv Lviv Kharkiv

not even their brother my father
who wanted us so badly to
assimilate and not stand out as

Ukrainian blood so that there
would be no prejudice no harassment
no racist jokes

so now as my aunts ranted
and raved I could understand
the neighbors on my street

my friends at school

strangers

racists

but I could not understand

I could never understand

my own family

assimilate 2

I

we stopped inviting Olena and Zaya
to Sunday dinner at the same time
one came one week the other the next

one came for Christmas
one for New Year's Day
one for Easter

Olena would attack on her Sundays
and continue the attacks on Zaya
during what she called the holy days

Zaya had no gossip in her
just a lament that began to
uncurl out of her like smoke

II

Olena she would say Zaya had
deserted her faith and become
a card-carrying Communist

had taken her son and husband
to Stalin's Ukraine where they found
only miles of dead under the snow

the thaws of spring sent screams
to Mary in heaven and a stink of blood
and skin that filled God's nostrils

Stalin's work but Zaya would not blame
her hero and forced her family to stay on
until the Nazis came and broke down the door

killed her husband killed her son took her
to Berlin to work in the war factories and
make bombs firearms tanks grenades

and flee the aircraft of America and Britain
and Canada that arrived like hawks and owls
and ripped up Berlin with their high explosives

oh Zaya would howl like a shot wolf
every November 11th fall to the pavement
and drench the cold with her pain

for that all of that Olena would not forgive
Mary would not forgive God would not forgive
but leave Zaya in the hells that had lured and deceived
her

III

Zaya she would drive me in her small car
dig from her purse a gray grainy photo
of a young man not unlike my brother

on the back a scrawl in fountain pen
blue-seeped into the paper she never
said anything about but knew I saw it

11

to my darling mommy he wrote
gifting her the photo of his
solemn face

my only son she wrote
lost
brokenhearted mother

IV

so Olena would try and turn us
against her sister while her sister
tried to show us her breaking point

all people like kindness but Zaya
so ached she would cry out in it gripping
you in a hug like a hard-muscled woman

and I was left to wonder what our family was
so far from Ukraine that father's grandfather's
country could split us apart cut sisters in two

I was left to wonder what else I did not know
what other stories had been hidden in hearts
and photographs and in Ukrainian syntax

what was the use of pretending we had
no past in Lviv or Ternopil or Kyiv
no stream of women children men

it was in us all around us
we had brought it here
it was in our houses and on every street

my sacred

I knew little of gods and seraphim
less of stained glass and light with
tips of fire I did not know Masses or
crucifixed choirs or anything of the
churches and sacred nothing of a sky-blue
heaven that threw light like splintered glass
I knew treed trees were holy greened grass
flow of brook clear rivers streams browned
with silt but I did not use that word or words like it
I did not call the spirit owl holy but I knew
who she was the stars of night she hunted by
I knew them by name I knew sunrise and
its fall and that it was our fall not the sun's I knew
all manner of beasts and rock and human struggle
they were my arteries my red copper sea
they were all
all of them
my sacred

mornings are magenta

who did not go to church was taken to church
male choirs groaning roiling at my back like
rough sea surge high banked thunderheads
of incense from a priest's fist images of
pale stretched faces long eyes impenetrable black

the home of my aunt my uncle a shrine of
dead eyes dead skin dead Jesus opening his
robes heart wrenched flame cutting thorn
my nostrils fill with incense in my room
great grandfather white and pepper black in
his coffin by the kitchen a large jar dark
green cucumbers float in brine in weeds
trout making their way through but avoiding
hook and line snapping their mouths
watching everything I do

we talk and eat they say thunder is

the rumble of the cart Satan uses to haul

souls to hell I go to my room to sleep

with the dead I wonder what color the dawn

will be if it has a color here

Mother of God

it became more important than eating lunch or supper

playing outside with my friends kicking the football

running till sweat made the skin peel wet off my bones

Ukrainians had killed Jews butchered them in pogroms

on Easter Sundays Orthodox priests turned

congregations loose to attack Jewish quarters and

slaughter Christ killers

this was god this was holy this was Jesus the Jew on the

cross I ran after the football I ran after a story any story I

could find where we saved Jewish girls and mothers

and did not strike them where we saved boys from their

brains skulls dreams smashed out against walls oh

Mother of God is there not a story where we were

human where their blood mattered to us

if you cannot find me that story then what good are
your Masses your candles your incense the icons the
prayers the long dark robes what good are your rituals
and liturgies who do they bless who help

I thought if at night I could drag Jesus off the cross and
hide him somewhere keep him out of sight so no one
would see him then the reason to massacre Jews would
be gone if I disappeared the one Jew the other Jews
would live the children live and their grandmothers and
uncles and pet cats whole worlds would exist and old
ones die in peace under the suns if I could just take Jesus
the Jew down off the cross hide him in my room
and keep him from climbing back up and hanging there
lifeless

deity

you promised me deity

but your road was never long enough for that

the journey too safe

the way too smooth

the outcome too predictable

you led me down a garden path

that was never dark enough

to see any god

I put away childish things

texts to gods and neighbors

I watch the images like you do
and avoid them like you do
I can switch to a hockey game
if I like or a movie on Netflix
one that is fast-paced filled
with action and hard violence
that is F/X

I cannot stop the war
even my prayers! I am
unable to see what they
change or don't change
just as thoughts and prayers
never stopped a lone wolf
shooter in America from
showing up and doing it
again

if I force myself to watch
I must stop before depression
sinks me like a stone in a
muddy creek

I may be able to convince myself
the whole damn war is another
conspiracy like the 2016 election
January 6 2021 COVID the vaccine
our hospitals are choked with
women and men dying and dead
from injections of Moderna or Pfizer
that Russia is the good guy in all this
and Putin an undiscovered
Mother Teresa

but it is too much it is beyond the pale
I can't do it leave me to myself
what difference does it make to see
I can't do anything you know I can't
how does it help me or the world
the world that mixes broken things

with happy ever afters tell me how it
matters to look at sunlight on the dead
blue skies over the slaughtered
larks in concentric circles over
children who should be watching them
and crying look look how many
how fast they fly running with their
small arms spread

I have sent checks and filled boxes
that have gone to Poland and over
the border into the smoke but
in the end I go home and life
is life I thank god it is mundane
I don't know what else to tell you
I don't know what else I can do or say
let's be blunt let's be transparent
let's not play at heroics I will have
my food and drink and peace

I'm all right Jack
my drawbridge is up

jeans

she brought a measure of peace
when family made no sense
their names and faces lost to me
when war Ukraine spilled blood
my ancestors my Cossack ponies
whetted swords fierce Mass candles
the crucified crucifying
when all the world was a twisting twine of
darkness and edged hard light

she came in jeans jean jacket top
brown hair making its way down her back
for years making its way with its plans
my best friend's sister three doors over
soothing all harms with a birthday kiss
lifting me away from gunfire
knots jagged shapes pricking far down
inside my chest lungs
far into my scarlet marrow

kissing as if she had spent her whole life

preparing for the moment she could love me

bring me peace and say softer than snow

you said it would never happen

yet here we are

you said it could never happen

but look at our fires and wildly spinning

sparks I've made you happy

you do not want me to stop

it had to be instinctual on her part

I knew she had done so little of this

or none of this

yet she understood how to kiss me

she knew how to make me surrender

to fairy tale beauty and a strong joy

a cloud drifting seagull lazy mind

the mythic princess taking hold of my spirit

with small white hands and wise lips

machines

I researched the second world war in the east
what Russia calls the Great Patriotic War
wanting to know what had happened
in Ukraine what battles had been fought there
what had happened to my father's and grandfather's
people my people

I found pictures of Russian tanks German tanks
T34s Tigers Panthers long black barrels
spewing dirty red fire I found Katyusha rockets
tearing apart the moon and sun like a meteor shower
homes with thatched roofs howling with flame
white black bodies flung on snow like trash

looking too long I could feel the thud in my bones
tanks blasted targets the earth shoving me back
the machines of a machine war lurched I lurched
could smell the stink of diesel and high explosive shells

could hear the fingernail screech of steel on steel the
shriek of armored wheels the shriek of crushed dead
crushed beneath

there was coffee hot blood hot
both cooling fast in morning wind soldiers laughing
because they have found sugar in thickest mud that
crawls and slimes up their boots to their knees cakes
their fingers paints their jaws and cheeks while all
around them are wrecked things wrecked tanks
wrecked aircraft wrecked machine guns wrecked
humans

but at some point no one sees no one feels and I
understood that to keep killing keep burning keep firing
rockets tank shells keep firing your rifle keeps breaking
bones and hearts sensation had to end mind had to stop
Jesus Buddha and all gods had to walk away and leave
you to yourself leave you to finish it finish what was left
of the war finish what was left of you

I walked away too walked away from my research
walked away from images on the iPod from film
of boiling smoke and body heaps black walked away
from the second world war only to find there was no
way away from war no way to end it that war came
again like winter

on TV the rockets
the tanks
the burnings
Ukraine a low dark cloud of
dead children raining down
raining on my eyes
my shoulders my back
raining on
my broken mind

goodbye Sergius of Radonezh

it was easy enough to give up Smirnoff

there are plenty of fine vodkas from

Latvia Ukraine and Lithuania

a bit harder to lay aside the Russian Orthodox

monks and saints and holy madmen but

they were no holier or unholier than me or others

always in bed with Tsars and Soviet strong men

and Russian dictators so I put aside their crosses and

icons and I take my own way from the way of the

pilgrim and if you think I am too harsh

tell that to the dead girl they murdered with rockets

I set aside all things Russian for this long winter
whether Tolstoy's novels or Chekhov's plays or
Yevtushenko's poems or Stravinsky's music
I set them aside along with any praise I have
rendered them any good wishes I have laid upon
their spirits any forbearance any grace
and if you think I am too harsh tell that to the dead girl
they murdered with rockets

if I must have Orthodox I have the Greeks and
Ukrainians if I must have Slavic novelists and poets
there are plenty in Ukraine in Poland Slovakia Czech
Croatia Slovenia Bosnia Herzegovina Macedonia
Slovenia Montenegro Bulgaria all of them I will set aside
the Serbs and the Belarus they have nothing to say to me
nothing that will bring strength to my heart and if you
think I am too harsh tell that to the dead girl they
murdered with rockets the girl who loved to sketch long
dark strokes in charcoal and form exquisite animals god
had never thought to create

midnight mass

a long wharf extended from the club far out into
lakewater dark milky dark smooth with few ripples
the moon ripe and hanging at the end of its branch
its round skingleam showing me a way across the subtle
tides if only I would walk it like a christ icon in its
brooding night of light and thick acrylic blackest bright
night

I stood on the wharf and wondered where good
nights went once they left taking moon and meteors
with them while the curving saxophone man in lean
slender black put out seductive notes as women in black
and diamonds wound and twined about the crowd at
the open bar and millionaire men in Italian suits
stepped out on the wharf to light cigars nod at the
author and laugh among themselves harsh laughter
which made me wonder if these Ukrainian men with
their diamond dark wives glistening glittering partners
long elegant lady friends were glad to be quit of the
Byzantine Jesus who hung by the door and watched

with eyes black with a billion years of infinity and
interstellar spaces everywhere they went everything
they did every look they left in the lowlit room with its
polished dance
floor boards and amber lights that made nothing easy to
see

the jazz player puts down his golden sax and sits still
to silvery shimmery walls of voices higher than Orion's
studded belt than Saturn's winging winding rings a
hymn to the cherubim Ukrainian singers never Russian
Belarus or Serbian Tchaikovsky wrote the music but
wars do that to artists and choirs and vocal intonations
if you are on the wrong side to those who remember
sides

I am not under the stars I am carried up among all
their different colors I once saw through a large lens in
an observatory and here I touch their firelight emeralds
topaz aquamarine garnet carnelian sapphire dazzled
and bewitched and blessed

I am lifted up beyond skies and atoms where
nothing material exists there is no matter no substance I
can measure or weigh or define there is nothing at all
and yet I am winged by something held by something
sustained by something other than nothing

the slender black and white jazzman and black
jazzman's jazz fingers strike the black and white keys
that strike the strings that string through worlds
vibrating harmonizing synthesizing till I am back on the
wharf pulled down to water and earth and hear two
ladies in night's black stars earrings necklace pendant
bracelet discussing my novel of the Ukrainian diaspora
how much the prize was worth I did not win how much
pleasure they took in its romance of the far away desires
of Kyiv and St. Petersburg clouds pearls and roses at
sunset they do not see me they are in the story I walk
past I am unknown one woman asks the other what did
you think of his human soul

the patriarch

if the rockets were killing Russian children

if the missiles were destroying Russian cities

if tanks were blasting Russian hospitals

all Russians not just the brave minority

would be crying for peace today

but it is not their children or houses or hospitals

so like Patriarch Kirill who leads the Russian Orthodox
Church

the Russian people support the invasion

and the killing of Ukrainian children

so long as it is not their own children

who have to suffer

beating heart

if god's hands did not know my hands
or his mind my thoughts jagged with black hurt
unstoppable gray rains and death masks
if god could not understand my cold winter night or the
end of all my faith
if the things that killed me were incomprehensible to
god because god was god and not human void of bones
and skin and blood and a beating heart how could you
ever say god was a god of love

a gathering of suns

I catch the falling stars

and make another universe

illuminated by constellations I configure

painting the night to story my own mythologies

no longer forcing myself to find a centaur in a Grecian

sky

but creating a zodiac of my own beasts and warriors

what I have unbelieved and what I could not un-exist

incandescence, my hauntings, angels that fell

a gathering of suns into images of misread destiny and

opaque infinities

that set my darkness ablaze

through a glass, darkly

Milwaukee

American Volunteer

treading the night

from Wisconsin rolling green over green
I came to Poland to Kyiv to rockets cracking open
buildings and bodies crunching glass and a
human's shin bones under our boots in the dark
nothing like stone desert and Taliban and
ragged yellow hills yet the Taliban had
fought the Russians too and driven them
to their knees

I am in cement and asphalt streets not
sand and gravel pits I see fires in the night
concrete sliced by a muscled missiled knife edge
water lines power lines sheared and scrambled
city snipers taking out legs feet arms snapping skulls
spreading blood in pools a Russian tank screeks scries
shrieks its steel around sharp corners and we kill it

a Javelin rocket makes it glow and die
taking all its men with it unless one or
two lucky out a hatch to curl on the
pavement we keep walking crouching
running through the night tracers are
shooting stars warfare constellations
Corporal Vasyl lights a cigarette flipping
the bird to snipers and says it is best to
fight in the night there are no visible wounds

war house 2022

I saw houses

where the only things moving

were shirts and pants pinned to a clothesline

flipping up and over in a blue sky wind

no people stood in the yards

no men bent over in gardens and weeded

no women hung dresses of yellow and pink on the lines

no children ran and tumbled over the green grass

past the windows and doors and locks

no breath no footsteps

no food steaming in pots

no music from radios or mobiles

when I walk past a war house

I know there are only the clothes in the wind

dresses and shirts turning around and around

around and around

black and bitter

we had this fire of scrap going among burning houses in
Kyiv and Myrrh was brewing Rocky Mountain coffee
plenty black from the marrow of the world Mother Q
Roast no one knew what the hell he was talking about
so we just shook our heads and laughed because why
not

his Uke Canuck life was different than I enjoyed
growing up in America I had pretty girls dancing with
their hair in ribbons flowers their embroidered blouses
and skirt and sexy thigh high red boots we had the
language and drunk uncles singing the language at
wedding receptions of a thousand where we drowned
in vodka and OJ

danced the hands on the others' hips polkas or the squat
on your ass Cossack kick out who the hell could do that
except guys with legs like semi-truck springs and
pounding diesel pistons ate the food we'd grown up

with kolbassa pyrohy holopchys plates piled high with
salami sauerkraut horseradish and for sure the borscht

where Myrrh said his father didn't want anyone to
know they had Ukrainian blood never talked about how
the family line had come from Lviv and Ternopil about
relatives who had returned and watched Stalin kill our
nation

I came to fight for Ukraine to make sure she stayed free
but with Myrrh I sensed there was something more that
it was not just about a rescue but about hard vengeance
about shedding cruel blood for cruel blood from a
hundred years before

Vasyl and Yana listened to our stories and wondered
about immigration and how the circle was unbroken
how the sons of the sons of the fathers and brothers and
mothers came back to fight for Ukraine maybe die and
bleed white on grease-stained asphalt their pockets
turned out by Russian scum for US dollars

they were Kyiv born lovers had taken Fine Arts degrees
both wanted to write scripts for TV and movies maybe
emigrate to LA or Vancouver write a novel or two on
the way what Slavic born are supposed to do they said
write out of black frost and wolves and bubbling
samovars unstoppable snowfalls stories known only if
chiseled into stone

this is us our squad crazy family fathers brothers
mothers BFFs lovers war brats chess masters Класно!
Cool! squad bodies with trident trinity triune god
patches lousy jokes Javelin handheld rocket launchers I
call American cigarettes hazardous to your health the
Surgeon General warns if you are from Putin's Moscow
another lousy joke but we laugh

Myrrh is still brewing coffee in a battered pot

"what do you call this shit" Vasyl gripes spitting it out

Myrrh laughs easy he doesn't give a goddamn if Vasyl
pushes him and says "back where all men are men and

women are stronger it's Dead Man Flats a midnight
mountain hard luck coffee few who are weak can drink
I just need some horseshoes to throw in some old saddle
leather a couple of double-oh-buck shotgun shells a
handful of steel nails that hurt going down a chopped
off thumb and we're all set squaddies"

"sounds like hell" Vasyl snaps

"you ought to know hell" Myrrh cuts back

Vasyl drinks three cups leaves it black and bitter even
though Yana found some sugar by a dead man's hand

no great loss

the bastards came to rape and pillage

we cut them down and left their smashed

bodies in missile holes and wreckage

their missiles their wreckage Leo and

Igor won't be going home to Murmansk

or Volgograd things went sour for the boys

no great loss

we sat in the dirt and the people in the town

gave us cold cooked cow tongue to eat

spiced with a bit of garlic something

different for me I was a little unsure

but hungrier than I was unsure

it tasted delicious

we are fighting on another street now

it was quiet so I went behind the house

the last house on the street that had

not been struck by missiles and

sat out of sight by a stream of water

I had no idea was there

no idea where it had come from or was going

silent flat shining like sheet metal

under a sheet metal sky

I tossed some pebbles into it and

made the trickle ripple and thought

my god children should be here tossing

these pebbles are all of them gone

are all of them completely gone one day

will we adults with our politics and

religions and protests and warfare

have erased them utterly from the earth?

I could stay here I could let the platoon

move on without me let them say I was

missing in action make the house a home

until its owners returned if they ever returned

if they were still alive keep house for them

ask a woman to be my wife a survivor hiding

in the rubble and ruins thinking it was better

to be here since lightning never struck twice

it would make quite a novel quite a movie

a volunteer comes from Milwaukee to fight

for freedom like his ancestors fought at

Lexington and he falls in love with a woman

whose hair is like early morning wheat eyes

the blue of July or August her figure fair and

strong a woman used to hard work in the fields

riding a John Deere but in Kyiv now to save her mother

yes it would be the Hallmark romance or a Harlequin or

better than that From Here to Eternity or Exodus played

out with Russia pouring fire upon us and clouds of

purple and black smoke obliterating the sun by day and

the moon by night yet she saves my life I save hers but

the mother is on a splintered street and she is a bag of

sticks holding onto a bag of sticks for firewood Tasha
picks her mother up broken and disjointed

buries her face in her mother's rags and bones and cold
skin weeps you can weep in a movie or novel but this is
not Hallmark now this is not Harlequin there is too
much that is too real and I wonder if Tolstoy would
write about the Russian invasion of Ukraine as he wrote
about the French invasion of Russia and whose side
would he take the invader's this time or would he hate
the blood shed at the desire of a mad Tsar and ply his
quill in the service of what is most human and the
innocent dead

yet our story hurries on I help Tasha harvest the rubble
and bring home canned borscht tins of tuna unbroken
bottles of Nemiroff and Mernaya vodkas some melted
butter eleven eggs unshattered a jug of milk garlic
pickles scattered across the roadway we pocketed
despite the dirt and grit we did not believe the war
would come back that it would end somewhere far

beyond the final Kyiv suburb maybe end at the border

my major concern was keeping up a fire of branches and

smashed beams from smashed homes helping Tasha

cook buckwheat

you'd think my imagination was strong enough to make

my story real my poem my fantasy my prayer you'd

think my mind might be strong enough to make the

streaming in my brain the stuff of which worlds

are made of and sustained and push out lifeless gutted

streets and replace them with my romance and the child

Tasha would womb and the child the child the many

childs she would birth the grass greening robins

returning the flowers mother of god the colors but Vasyl

the corporal walked through it all through the thin

stream in his muddy boots and said let's go Milwaukee

we are fighting on another street now

Vasyl

Ukrainian Army

a perfect target

the light through broken glass
made him a perfect target
I could see every hair in his beard
even with just the iron sights see
every tooth in his head every freckle
on his cheek nothing else said Ivan
Stravinsky like his red splotchy freckles

they said he was related to the great composer
I never asked we were too busy fighting for
the puck or jostling in front of the net or slamming
one another into the boards though we never
dropped our gloves never punched the other's
face bloody never crosschecked or high sticked
just played rough hockey the way rough hockey is
played

even when it wasn't Russia against Ukraine we

were never on the same side always in different

jerseys lining up on opposite sides of the rink

facing off against each other staring each other

down shaking each other's gloves at the end

without looking one another in the eye just

going back to our lives without the other in it

so now the light through broken glass

made Ivan Stravinsky a perfect target

I could see every hair in his beard

even with just the iron sights see

every tooth in his head every freckle

on his cheek nothing else said Ivan

Stravinsky like his red splotchy freckles

I put a bullet through his brain

Marlboro Reds

it will sound cliché but I gave the captured Russ some
American chewing gum I had in my pocket   chiclets
in an old yellow package that were glued together god
help me there was even some lint fuzz but he took them
and popped them in his mouth   I asked if he smoked
he didn't but wanted a cigarette anyways   we had a
devil of a time getting both our Marlboro Reds lit in the
wind and burnt our hands cupped about the Zippo but
you could say it was worth it just to sit on the tank a
minute and smoke together instead of pointing AK-74s
at one another's eyeballs   he actually found some
laughter in his chest and joked he was a cowboy
smoking a Marlboro for the first time in his life   I
made sure he got a plateful of perogies and that no one
photographed it to use for propaganda so others
couldn't say I only fed him for that reason   he had
bailed as the Javelin struck his T-80 and another tanker
had fallen from a hatch but was killed in the blast   his
whole crew was gone   he did not talk about it   I let
him use my mobile to call his mother to tell her he was

alive   a medic checked him over he only had a few

scrapes and bumps   he snubbed out his cigarette

between his fingers before it was done and dropped the

butt into his shirt pocket buttoning it   until next time

he said to me

we were born for this

I don't know who it was that made the first video of us
with a soundtrack of born for this by The Score
blasting   rockets scratching out fast flame   tanks
decapitated   we're pumped   finally free to fight
instead of waiting for Russia waiting for Russia   our
friends are grinning   all in camo our rifles are
black   they are always black   they've been fired in
anger   yes for sure there is anger in the video even
though it was meant to be upbeat   the explosions are
angry   yellow and red tracers are angry   I may be
smiling Yana may be smiling but we crackle with anger
like sticks in a fire pit   I guess we were psyched when
Roman or Peter filmed the video   patched it together
with ripped music   showed it to us   sent it to
mom   a girlfriend or two   Roman had one in
Romania   another in Ternopil   we felt good we felt
strong   able to hold our own against Russia the
Kremlin Putin the T80 tanks with their ugly snouts the
Su-27 jets with their kill bill rockets   a bit invincible
Peter said lighting his American cigarettes   where did

he get them from   just enough of the invincible to
give Ivan hard stone migraines and the thick bitter bile
at the back of the throat no one wants   you were born
for this   your parents were lovers who conceived you
for this   god brought you to life for this   you are a
tall green tree for this   but I do not watch the video
anymore   I deleted it from my mobile   how many
in the clip are still with us two weeks later   Peter is in
a hospital in Kyiv   Andrii we don't know where he is
or what happened to him   Roman is dead   Anna is
dead   Jack who came to Ukraine from Canada five
years ago is dead   the major called it a lucky missile
strike   I asked him who was lucky

smoke

this is different
I don't care what color it is
this is not campfire smoke
no one laughs around this smoke

this is not fire pit smoke
no one sits and roasts garlic sausage here
no one has beer or vodka or a cooler
no one eats and drinks around this smoke

this is not fireplace smoke or wood stove smoke
this does not go up any chimney or metal pipe
no one puts up their feet and has a cigar or cigarette
no one takes it easy and feels good around this smoke

this is the smoke of fires that gain flame from human
skin that only days ago fought fear prayed they would
survive looked forward to Easter to Pascha to April
poppies yes thank god I will see red poppies I know I
will see them

this smoke is different

it is the smoke of dead homes and dead fences

it is the smoke of hard journeys and hard endings

it is the smoke of Russians and Ukrainians

it is the smoke of Gogol

the bitter black smoke of Gogol and all his dead souls

blood roots

it was after we found the executions   so many ages
ages on top of ages crunched into shallow pits   it
looked to us like grandsons bled bone white with
grandfathers   mothers staring wild-eyed at daughters
as they suddenly left the earth   Yana went into a funk
and wouldn't talk   everyone around us was singing
the red viburnum in the meadow in defiance of Russia
and the invasion   even soldiers   *oi u luzi chervona*
kalyna   червона калина на лузі   a first world war
song written for our Sich Riflemen in the bleak gray
days which had returned in black and blood   Pink
Floyd covered it with Andriy Khlyvnyuk of Boombox
Yana and I learned it when we were kids   *in the*
meadow a crimson kalyna is bent down low   she was
furious with Milwaukee and Myrrh for not knowing the
song   she threw her helmet across the broken room
we were sheltered in shouted I thought you were
Ukrainian in your damn veins   I told Myrrh and
Milwaukee the kalyna was a national symbol   it was
about loyalty to the ancestral homeland   blood roots

Selah from a kibbutz near Hatzor had carried her guitar
into battle which we all thought was nuts   she
brought it out and strummed   demanded I teach the
song to the volunteers who she called *mitnavim*   I am
no Andriy Khlyvnyuk   Yana stayed dark until I
began   we croaked along   Milwaukee was
especially terrible his voice like a goat's   Yana joined
in on our third try pitch perfect dragging us along with
her and Selah   she asked if it was wrong for a Fine
Arts grad to write a soft poem shaped by petals and sun
on her skin and knife cut heartbreak   I shrugged
who am I the god of rhymes   if your heart is in it and
you can form impressions that strike with the paint on
your fingers then it's art   it won't rhyme she said but
I want it to talk   she worked on it an hour maybe two
I lost track of her   she gave me the page ripped and
scattered with dirt   she had written it in English   I
did not say anything after I'd read it twice because we
were attacked   I crammed it in my pocket and went
out into the fire

where children fall

where bodies fall wildflowers break through
streams run clear and wide lakes are silver
grasses turn from winter's browns to find green light
sunflowers take root and fireflame poppies burst

where children fall the wind is softer for that
the north wind does not come or if it must
it leaves quickly letting the south wind have its way the
cold wind does not linger the cold wind remembers

where mothers fall the earth is soon black and rich
chernozem that can grow any crop grow wheat
corn barley and give out fast rivers of sunflower's sweet
oils even though there is war we sow seed and believe
in it

where people fall in their youth and in their ripening years the sun does not disappear the rainclouds come and go snow falls and snow melts and ice skies are soon April death does not end anything all the souls still live and breathe

where bodies fall the land lives and breathes with them souls are luminous in the world we cannot imagine or create in paint poems or dance while we ourselves find there are new days to live many children to be born

it rises at one end of the heavens

the snow melted back
and bodies melted back with it
black frosted and lost since winter

identified tagged buried family notified
spring still came on it was not stopped
by heartbreak decay war weapons hatred

you cannot stop spring or grass greening
cannot stop sunrise or sunset or moons
cannot kill beauty or the seasons or the wind

I drank in the air it was fresh sharp
like a white wine cold in the hand
you could get drunk on the air

hey Yana I said the sun rises like a
gold coin from my pocket if only I
had one it rises at one end of the heavens

just like the Holy Bible says moves west

and sets like a bonfire so many colors

we still have our sunsets we have sunrise

yes she said

but what are they good for

Yana

Ukrainian Army

blackest night

neither of us wanted much   it was enough to stare up
at the extreme blackness of a new moon and let it absorb
us completely   it pulled us right up into it and it was
good   Vasyl's head on my chest my arm across his
and clasping his hand with all the silver rings on
mine   I think it was ten minutes that went by perhaps
twelve or thirteen where there were no white scars of
rocket strikes   no jagged orange and red on the
horizon that told us a house was burning out of control
an apartment complex a hospital   no parabolas of
colored tracers that could be fireworks   fireworks in
times of peace that could make me gasp with pleasure
and crush Vasyl's fingers in my grip   the black took
away talk   our kisses were random   we just
wanted to look at darkness   at what was
lightless   no faces illuminated by cigarettes   no
mobiles or watches   what are stars like   when does

the sun rise   when is it daylight   we wanted to
forget

the rings of Saturn

the birds would screech and fly up with the gunfire
the red Vesuvius of Saint Javelin cracking a Russian
tank open blasting it and its Russian souls all to hell and
perdition

after the killing roads and highways of slaughter
the birds return I hear tunes a rhythm a bursting of
notes while shell smoke hazes and copper blood stings
nostrils

even the crows sound better than machine guns and
rockets and larks don't belong here not now not today
not this life I feed a sparrow a bit of bread and I said
you should go little soul

sometimes I wonder why they bother coming back

why don't they wing to another country or cross the sea

seek an alternate universe find a wormhole and dive in

maybe go to another planet maybe the rings of

Saturn maybe just a better wheat field in Romania or

Poland

can't god give them a better life

gone to graveyards

Max was the best butcher cured the best hams at his
own smokehouse
loved his vodka and his beer and his wife of twenty
years but he too
picked up the gun when the dark wolf crept to his door

Maria was a beauty queen had won many prizes for her
looks and a mind
like a Swiss watch poems like blistering ruby gems but
she too
picked up the gun when the dark wolf crept to her door

Anna had fifteen children all untiringly loved ran her
home like a ship on the Atlantic
staying its course in wind and hail in light too bright to
see but she too
picked up the gun when the dark wolf crept to her door

Andrii liked nothing better than his violin his church his
gods his vodka

his lady friends who never tired of his humor or his

smile of many pearls but he too

picked up the gun when the dark wolf crept to his door

and the doors of his ladies

now they friendship together in a mass grave

no distinction between them the Russians

in a hurry to bury and run

doll within doll

Orthodox within saint

son of David have many many mercies

on me a sinner a sinner many times over a sinner

unholy Mother Russia ran and ran by day

and by night she ran she did not want to be caught

by moon or sun's suns or heaven's sacred stars did

not want to be caught in her most lurid moment with

the bleedings of other's bleedings on her white pure

bible paper hands thin white bible paper hands with

their gilt edges

jigsaw

I just needed something else   I tugged Vasyl away
from the squad to where flickers were walking a dead
Russian tank and strong loved him   put everything
in   everything harsh edged painful   put all parts of
my mind and thinking the sharp internal
bleedings   while tank candlelight jigsawed his face
and made him different people all the different people
inside him   and brought out all my different people
too so that everyone was seen everyone known
everyone everything given skinfire that warmed us
without needing the adrenaline rush of fast
killings   because warcut left puzzle pieces of
indifference strewn over our limbs   love stroke was
better   Vasyl had to have his cigarette afterward just
like he did after combat   I used to like to smoke and
watch him sleep after our lovestorms   I'd take
everything out of him but I put a lot in too   fair trade
I called it   making him smile over the bitter wake up
coffees he favored   but that was before the
war   there was no time to sleep now or watch

someone sleep or tease them or flirt and no time for me
to smoke unless I got my hands on American cigarettes
from Milwaukee and then I made time   one child had
its DOB blood type allergies phone numbers names
addresses of family on the skin of her back in permanent
marker   it had not saved her   I put my cold
weather jacket over her thin body and its lines of
ribs   she came to me in my stormswept brain after
Vasyl's love or after sleep so that I hated waking
up   everyone remained alive when I was in REM
sleep   but hauntings or no hauntings I had to have
the good strength of Vasyl's body or nothing made
sense to me   someone put a note by an enemy
paratrooper's body   I had shot him the day before
and he was still scrunched up against the wall of the
church   they scratched out a note and left it on his
shoulder   росіянин убив росіянина   *see a Russian
kill a Russian*   someone had added in red   За
любов марії і наших дітей вбивають росіянина   *for
the love of Mary and our children kill a Russian*   I
wondered if the split tank giving us candlelight would
blow up while we sat there   I might have cared in

February I didn't care now   I doubted the T80 would
do anything but burn down into grunge and greasy
ash   I heard Myrrh laughing and realized that now I
needed his laughter as much as I'd needed Vasyl to
need me   I dressed and laughed myself because I
wasn't even cold and I'm always cold even on a Kyiv
summer day   what is that   I laced my black
boots   I'd felt Vasyl's eyes on me the entire time but
pretended he had no effect on me   which he
understood   Yana you are a different kind of human I
have to confess it's not so easy to get to know you   I
shrugged tightened my web belt picked up my
gun   who is

Myrrh

Canadian Volunteer

corrosive

from Afghanistan to Canada to Europe
I walk across borders in the head and in the soil
embedded with other volunteers from every
point of the compass and embedded with a
frontline Ukrainian Army unit our corporal
calls The Mixed Blessing his stained tooth
laugh Orthodox Cross swinging from his neck
like a gibbet tobacco stained fingers for guns
and prayer

those first nights were asphalt
fresh laid black I could not see
outside the wire had been
like that in the sandbox Afghanistan
but this was not the same this was a
different dark an urban dark

somehow that made it the

River Styx impenetrable

yet I found targets one after

another I popped heads in

the dark took out hearts in

the dark shattered chests and

Russian dreams after the war

he thought I will marry and

move to St. Petersburg but now

you are asphalt dark on asphalt

I did this to you I was always

a good shot on deer elk and

black bear I was a good

mankiller in the desert

now I am good at snuffing boys

from Moscow Kazan Samara Perm

I kill them often I kill them

quickly I say to them as I shoot

checkmate!

it does not bother me they kill

so much I kill so much it is right

it is the balance and acid rock rhythm

of war but when I wake in cold dark

I feel my soul falling away there is

a gnawing in my brain and guts

something immortal is disintegrating

I erode like a shoreline

break small like the edges of a road

like a human watch left in the rain

with its multiple functions and

electronic oscillator its quartz crystal

movement and order of magnitude

hands and components intact precise

in synch as I sight trigger and fire

I corrode

temple

I looked down at the twisted Russian body with the
cross twisted around its neck on a silver chain   blood
drenched uniform white skin white bone jabbing
through   he had come to kill us in the name of god
his religion gave the yes to war slavery and cruelty
his bible was a savage book   brutality lurked behind
protestations of eternal love   the genocidal god tried
at The Hague for crimes against humanity   god the
war criminal   ordering Israel to wipe out their
enemies kill every last one   kill the children slaughter
the infants murder the babies nursing at their mother's
breasts and murder the mothers too   kill all the
animals all the livestock   but keep enough alive so
you can keep calm and carry on sacrificing to me
god dictated those bible pages women and men put
words in his mouth   generation after generation take
their darkness at face value   Christ rejected the
tyrannical god   you have heard it said   heard it
read   hate your enemies eye for eye tooth for tooth
but I say love   walk among the ironclad religious

commit to love over against the tyrannical god as Christ

committed to love over against the tyrannical god and

the fires of heresy are hungry for you   fires of war the

Orthodox of Russia carried to us in long black robes just

as their cold god trapped in snow and ice commanded

if I wanted to dip into the black bible's poems of cries I

could always do that   the poems of cries were all

around me rising with the fires and screams   I

wanted to kill the Orthodox for what they believed

do I not hate those who hate you do I not loathe those

who rise up against you I hate them with complete

hatred I count them my enemies   I killed many please

war god I will kill many more   many more Russians

with their silver crosses twisted at their throats   burn

in hell priest we fight for our souls and all the love and

beauty in them   we do not need anything from a

Russian god who lives and sleeps in a temple in

Moscow

after the Russian retreat

there, mother, I will set you just so
the sun is already warm, it is spring after all
the wall has baked in the heat for hours
your back will feel wonderful, your bones
not so stiff, almost like new

there, mother, let me make sure you are comfortable
something to eat? something to drink?
I forget myself, I'm sorry, I need to remember what is
going on food and drink don't matter to you when you
are so tired and only want to close your eyes

there, mother, I can straighten your legs for you
is that better? is that where you want your arms?
how about your babushka? does it keep out the wind?
and your skirt, let me help you tuck it under your legs
that way the grit and gravel of the street will not bite

there, mother, you look well, perhaps a pillow

a pillow can work wonders, right between your head

and the wall, a nice cushion, something soft

so, now you are ready, now I will close your eyes for

you

close your eyes finally so you can sleep

sleep, mother, sleep forever

Bucha

I need a cello

the violin will not help

no matter how well played

no matter how painful

the twisted strings

no human's voice is dark enough

there is no place here for trumpets

no place for accordians or drums

I need a cello

a cello can reach the black hole

of the fragmentation

a black hole

that disassembles all souls

an oubliette where the strange way in or out

is a trap door in the ceiling of the stars

opening to nothing

hands tied behind backs

shot in the head

shot between the eyes

hooded tortured raped

screams

still ringing through the planets

ringing Saturn ringing the universe

there is no end to the crying of

crying blood in the ground and

crying among meteors and our infinities

Bucha sounds like Buchenwald

Did you think of that before you

Murdered human and called it Russia

Russia of Tolstoy and the Bolshoi

Russia of Shostakovich

Russia of the Cherry Orchard

of Yevtushenko's Babi Yar

did you think of that before you became

werewolf

Bucha 2 (the flower of Guernica)
It's not history that repeats itself. It's violence.

Picasso's Guernica has one terrified hand clutching onto
a flower the mud grit and exhumed rot in Bucha have
no hands that can hold onto anything

we unearth maggots a woman nearby tells us a Russian
soldier demanded cigarettes from her husband he did
not have any the soldier shot him in the head he
dropped at her feet

she could not grasp the moment it was not something
she had ever thought to conceive she fell to her knees
took his head and blood into her lap but he had left
behind only his soft face

my relative whose husband was shot by Nazis in
Ukraine fell at his wife's feet before she could blink they
shot her son her only son her only child and let him fall
too

the woman smokes a Camel I gave her and watches our

digging go on watches waits for her husband to return

re-emerge open his eyes smile I only pretended to be

dead

face to face

ice skater

yet sometimes among shattered bodies

sometimes some days I turn as an ice skater turns

a full circle and in that smooth swinging

swoop everything has changed where there

was blackened heath and a steppe of rough

dirt and murdered hearts strewn like shattered

rock rise grasses and wheat stalks the grasses

a shining green like the tropics and the

rainforest the wheat a sunrise of its own

spreading over fields I can see and

beyond them to fields I cannot count so

I cannot help but wonder these people prayed

to a god that they might defeat Russia and

never thought a god was myth or

that resurrection and rebirth of Ukraine would

not come I see them stretch for breath and strength

they want to make love again and kiss warm skin

gargoyle

I see an empty supernatural I have
no eyes for gods devils loaves and
fishes heavens demoniacs chained
tongues of flame dancing spring
morning resurrections white lilies

Vasyl with his long silver Orthodox
Cross swinging from his neck a cross
just like our enemy dead wear laid shoulder
to shoulder in snow splashed by gray road spray
blood and stones visited by April's larks

kneeling in the dirt of this shattered
house where we eat and sleep I see him
by a window splintered into razor triangles
rocketfire blast a halo about his head and
grizzled unshaven jaw Saint Vasyl the
not so great bent over kissing the cross

his lips move his fists whiten blood gone
is he praying for his own survival for all
of us to live again does he pray for Kyiv
Mariupol Kharkiv for his enemies Putin in his
Machiavellian cut Brioni suit Vitaliano tie
washing down raw oysters with iced Smirnoff

tears stumble and stutter along his face his
whole body quivers do you see god
is god cheerful or thorned is there kindness in the
eyes or thunderheads building with hail and
retribution what puts heart into you Vasyl what
puts a kind of faith in when a faith just like it devours us

Vasyl looks up at me his mouth like a shell fragment
features rinsed by explosions and the dark that
hurries back after each burst of fast hard light
you think it is nothing Myrrh it is foolish but my
tattered skin and bone prayers carry the earth on their
backs green worlds you cannot count where good life
bristles and is strong

where prayers ignite darkfall and make the black
incandescent they create a holy fire savage enough
to see a skin ten-fingered blooded god face to face

the pieces of a human

The breaking of a heart I found on the asphalt and
hatred was very much like it on the ground where I put
it with my gun.

My words my pale words that have no connections I
wish my words were incantations I wish they had such
power that when I spoke they made things exist they
made peace emerge out of flaming streets they forced
invaders to withdraw they closed every wound sutured
every soul.

The last Russian I killed in Kyiv fell under an icon of
Christ the icon was on a single wall facing the road the
rest of the building was gone there was just the jagged
wall and the icon with its lost eyes looking at the dead
Russian.

Yana has the puppy she found cowering under a
staircase that had no house Vasyl is trying to get us all
in the truck to Donbas and Milwaukee is using his

spoon on a can of beans he opened with his bayonet almost cutting apart his hand.

We go to kill those who kill us just as we killed them in Kyiv the killing that will never stop until the Russians leave the killing that will go and on if the Russians stay and I know the killing that will come to their cities and streets just as darkness gives way to more darkness long before there is a hint of sun.

You think it will always go your way Ivan that it will always be our children and families who die while yours remain safe miles away snug in their beds happy at the breakfast table free to roam their streets without the fury of missiles and gunfire.

But it will come Ivan as it came to the Nazis who invaded your country it will come to you who invaded ours as it came to Berlin it will come to Moscow as you brought horror to our infants and our young it will come to yours and shatter them like bright panes of window glass.

Once a war is begun it spreads like a fast hard river
breaking its banks upon everyone upon you Russians
upon all your people the floods will come upon you
who killed us will come what kills you every penny
must be paid out every scorched daughter answered for
every rape every torture every spill of blood on grass
and city street.

The truck is bringing us to you the icons in our pockets
are coming to the icons in your pockets the bullets in
our guns are coming to the bullets in your guns the
death in your eyes will look into the death in ours you
will not withdraw we will not surrender our lives
collide.

Milwaukee cleans the dirt from under his fingernails
with a knife tip but the knife is too big Vasyl smokes his
Marlboro Reds and talks about owning a ranch and
raising Black Angus while he rides a black horse Yana
strokes the puppy in her lap and says she will find a
safe place for him in Donbas while she kills every

Russian she sees I watch them turn into fire after fire as the sunlight makes its way into the back of the truck.

Remember Lady Macbeth?

What about Lady Macbeth?

I don't think I can get this blood out of my skin. I've been trying. Soap does no good. I've been rubbing and rubbing. Soon I'm going to be taking the skin off right next to the bone.

Orthodox Easter
A Ukrainian soldier in the Donbas

I had a tin of sardines for Easter they were good
sardines
Someone told us Putin had attended Midnight Mass
We laughed and said we'd know he meant it
If the Russian army and its mercenaries were gone in
the morning

For some faith is thicker than politics
For others politics is thicker than faith and blood
And they prove it by shedding so much of it
The Russians were still there in the morning

Orthodox Easter 2

A Ukrainian soldier in the Donbas

The Russians didn't neglect an Easter greeting

An hour before dawn they filled the dark with

Bright tracers lit us up with missiles and rockets

A celebration of sound and fire

Near our base a missile implanted itself in the grass

It had not exploded its tail was sticking out of the soil

They had scrawled Христос воскрес on it

Christ is risen

the Donbas ritual

war cannot change even when seasons change even
when you go from cities to grasslands to small forests
and hillsides where men die among spring flowers of
white and yellow with their green stems tiny ants and
aphids crawling over stiff fingers with mud under their
nails

war cannot change tanks swoop over the steppe like
Nazi tanks did like Soviet tanks did like a hawk hunting
for rabbits BTR-80s T-72s T-64s burn out dark just as
tanks did at the northern front of Kyiv just as they do
everywhere on earth in Yemen in Syria they burn the
same way are the same shade of black their steel
ruptures like an internal organ ripped by a 7.62x39mm
bullet a 5.45x39mm bullet any bullet you press down
into a magazine and snap into a rifle

war cannot change bodies break like bodies broke under
Viking axes under the sharp hooves of Roman cavalry
under scimitars at the walls of Jerusalem under javelins

hurled by the Macedonians under arrows fired by
English longbows at Agincourt the French knights
tumbling to earth and dying in the dirt as we die in the
dirt die the same way look the same as war dead ever
looked from the Stone Age to the age of steel to the age
of missiles rockets and killer drones

woke one colding dawn out of a rirling of dreams and
night terrors saw a grassy field strewn with broken
spears pennants dragging in mud puddles dying horse
shattering blades burning black shields crackling
crumbling castles white Russians chess pieces scattered
among weeds and thistles shining black crows feeding

war cannot change we fight to resist extinction the
enemy fight to conquer our rigid bodies are the same
our blood our wounds no different the bewildered wild
dead eyes but this is the Donbas ritual this is how we
secure our freedom bolt cutters blue-tipped acetylene
torches we cut through skin and bone and steel and
bring life to an end like a god

a dark Mariupol dark

I walk dark in dark
streets dark buildings dark
birds dark on their backs
dogs cats horses all dark
humans dark
children dark
dark in dark
in the dark Russian heart

acknowledgements

The following poems originally appeared in a slightly different form in the book Petals published in 2016 by MillerWords as part of the Zo series on Russia and Ukraine. Used with permission: colors, beating heart, war house 2022.

My thanks to Suz Deshchidn who spent many hours on the manuscript to help shape it into its final form, to Mary Rumford who crafted a brilliant cover front and back, to Marvin Brauer who believed in me enough to give me the opportunity to write these poems about a people and a war and their longing for freedom and peace. May you all be blessed with light and life.